Happy
Holidays

Written and illustrated by Alix Wood

My thanks to
Rebecca Wood,
Clellan and Brennan Bray
and Kevin and Ben Wood
for their help with this book

Published by Truran

© Alix Wood 2006

Editorial consultant Tina Bray

This reprint 2013

ISBN 978 185022 210 1

Truran is an imprint of Tor Mark,
United Downs Industrial Estate, St Day,
Redruth, Cornwall TR16 5HY

www.truranbooks.co.uk

Printed and bound by R Booth Ltd,
The Praze, Penryn, Cornwall TR10 8AA

Contents

Introduction

Happy Holidays is packed full of ideas to entertain your family; arranged in five chapters: on a walk, on a car journey, on the beach, in the garden, and on a rainy day. You're sure to find something to do wherever you are.

Most of the ideas are fun for all the family. Look out for these symbols which indicate that I've tried out these activities with teens and toddlers – successfully.

On a walk

Find a clearing with a few trees. Blindfold one person, spin them a couple of times and lead them to a tree. They have to feel the tree and get to 'know' it. Lead them back to the middle of clearing and then get them to guess which was their tree.

Blindfold Challenge

Blindfold one person and slowly lead them across an obstacle course using only verbal commands. Very funny, and particularly good at teaching left and right. Perhaps give a prize to the 'director' if they direct another to the end unharmed! Or forget the obstacle course and direct the person to an object to 'fetch' instead.

Follow my Leader

TODDLER
0-3
APPROVED

Great fun for the very young. Go over and under obstacles following the leader. Can you fit through the same gaps as your three year old? Try hopping, walking sideways, twirling round, or shouting out silly words.

Bird Tracks

Swan

Goose

Duck

See if you can find any of these footprints by the water's edge. They are actual size.

TRY THIS!

If your children are flagging on a long walk, try these tips. The first to find an item eg five different leaves, gets a prize. Or play boo, one adult runs ahead and hides behind a tree. Toddler has to run and find them before they jump out and shout boo.

Animal Tracks

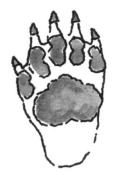

Badger

A badger track has five toes and a large kidney-shaped pad. Badgers use the same paths over and over. You may find their coarse white-tipped hairs caught on fences or brambles.

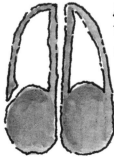

Otter

Tracks by a river or waterway may be an otter. They have five toes with an almost round pad. In soft mud you might see evidence of webbing between the toes.

Fox

The fox does not keep to regular trails. A fox track is very like a dog's, but smaller. The print has four toes with the outer two curving inward.

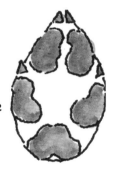

Deer

Deer have cloven hooves.

Rat   **Squirrel**   **Rabbit**

Rat, squirrel and rabbit are found near their burrows or feeding areas. Rabbit tracks have two little tracks for the front paws with two long tracks for the back legs.

Orienteering

One person makes a trail for the others to follow. Perhaps bury some treasure at the end, or have the picnic lunch set up there. A simple trail can be made by dropping bits of bread or stones. You can make fallen twigs into arrows and lay them on the paths, or tie string to branches. To make it really hard for older children, use stones as markers or tie tall grasses into a knot.

Here are some signs that you could use

This is the trail   Turn right   Turn left

This is the trail   Turn right   Turn left

This is the trail   Turn right

Turn left

TRY THIS!

TODDLER 0-3 APPROVED

Everyone knows Hide and Seek, but have you tried it with the family dog. Make the dog sit and stay, and sniff a dog chew. Then take the chew and hide it. See how fast the dog can find it. You could try and see if he could find an old sock instead.

Make a shelter

Most wooded areas will have lots of fallen twigs and branches that can be made into shelters. You can make a teepee by leaning bigger branches up against a tree trunk, or make a shelter under an over-hanging branch. Make sure the branches aren't so big that they would hurt if they fell on you.

You can make an 'A' frame shelter if you have some string, and perhaps thatch it with leaves or long grass. Bracken or grass makes a nice mattress inside the shelter too.

Don't damage any trees or plants, and dismantle your shelter when you leave.

Bow and Arrow

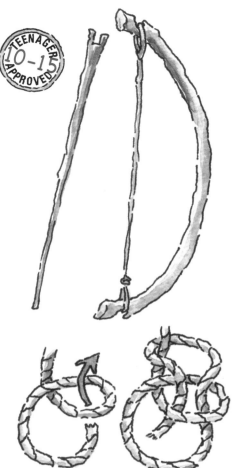

Make your bow with a long supple branch, thin enough to bend, but with difficulty. Ask an adult to cut a notch in both ends with a strong knife. Get a piece of string a little longer than the bow, and tie a loop in each end. Use the knot below to make a loop which doesn't slip. Bend the branch and slip the loops into the notches, make the string really taut. Make the arrow from a long straight twig. Notch the thicker end. Put the notched end onto the string when you shoot. Never point the arrow at a person or an animal.

Bowline knot

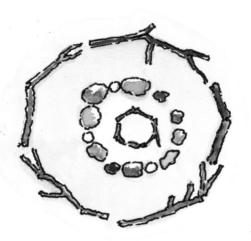

Make a target

Create concentric circles out of sticks or stones on the ground. Toss a stone from a distance and see who scores a bull's eye. Or shoot arrows from your bow.

10

Hopscotch

Revive the game of hopscotch! Draw out a court with a stick in the earth. If you've forgotten the rules here they are. Toss a marker into the first square. It must land completely within the square. The player hops through the court beginning on square one. Straddle side by side squares. Single squares are hopped on one foot. When you reach the end of the court, turn round and hop back, stopping to pick up the marker on the way. If successful, move to square number two. If the player throws to the wrong square, steps on a line, misses a square, or loses balance, the turn ends. The first player to complete one to ten wins the game.

Scavenger hunt

Give each person a plastic bag and a list of things to find. The first one home with the most items wins. It's a good idea to include a 'longest' or 'smallest' to make sure there is a clear winner.

A woodland walk list could include a pinecone; four different leaves; a stone; longest piece of grass; an acorn; a feather or a snail shell, for example.

TRY THIS!

TODDLER
0–3
APPROVED

Draw the items instead for a toddler scavenger hunt.

Plastic bag kite

All you need is a plastic bag, two sticks and a length of string. Tie the sticks in a cross shape firmly, as shown.

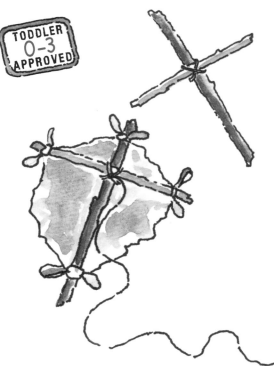

TODDLER 0–3 APPROVED

Tie a corner of the bag to each end of the cross. Tie a long bit of string to the centre of the cross, and there you have your simple kite. If you run fast and drag it along behind you it should lift into the air.

Flip a coin walk

Transform an ordinary walk with your children into an extraordinary adventure. Flip a coin. If it lands on tails your walk starts by turning left. If it's heads, turn right. Continue doing this at every corner. You never know where you'll end up! Try and keep track so you can get home though! This is most fun in the town.

TRY THIS!

Try the 'One Minute Walk'. Draw a finishing line and a start line. Everyone must walk forward for exactly one minute. If you reach the finish line you must keep going and not turn around. You also can't stop. The one nearest the finish when the time is up wins the game.

Crafts from finds

Acorn Mouse

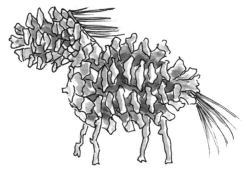

A simple model to make with young ones is a mouse from an acorn. The acorn is the body and if you find one with the stem that makes a perfect tail. You can glue on cardboard ears (pva glue works best) and paint on eyes and whiskers.

Pine Cone Pony

Glue four straight twig legs to a pinecone body. For the head and neck, glue a small pinecone to the end of a twig covered in pine needles. Trim the needles to make a spiky mane, then glue the head to the body. Stick a thick bunch of pine needles to the back to make the tail.

Fairy Camps

Collect leaves and twigs. Stick the twigs in the earth in a semicircle. Get a few long bendy twigs and tie them together to make a roof. Cover the roof with leaves, and make a floor with grass. To make a bed out of twigs, take two longer twigs and two short twigs and tie them with string at the corners to make a rectangle. Take two bendy twigs and tie them to the rectangle to make the ends and legs. Weave grass around to make the base, and make bedding out of leaves.

Fairy Chair

Collect twigs, one long, bendy piece that will form the back legs and back, and eight equal length twigs for the two front legs, the middle back and the seat. To make the back, bend the long twig, and tie one of the smaller pieces in between the two ends the height you want the seat to be. Then tie on the sides of the seat. Next tie the front piece of the seat to these side twigs, then tie the two front legs and trim the chair legs even. Add sticks to the middle of the back and the seat and weave grasses as shown. Maybe decorate the top with a daisy. You could put the chair in the woods for the fairies to use.

TRY THIS!

Make a tree from bark rubbing and leaf prints. Take a large sheet of paper, lining paper is ideal, and draw the outline of a thick trunk and branches. Place the paper on a tree trunk and rub over the bark with a brown crayon to make the trunk and branches textured. Then collect some leaves. Back at home, paint the leaves on one side different autumn colours, and gently press on the paper around the trunks to create leaf prints.

On a car journey

One child draws a map of a journey with pictures of things they see along the way. The other children have to spot all the things on the way back. This is particularly helpful to spice up a regular boring journey like the school run or a trip to a relative.

Name Link

Say a name and the next player uses either the first or last name to make another one. For example, it could go Hugh Grant, Hugh Laurie, Laurie Lee, Lee Evans and so on. Perhaps give a forfeit to anyone who can't go.

TEENAGER 10-15 APPROVED

Animals

TODDLER 0-3 APPROVED

Everyone looks out of the car and tries to spot animals. You get a point for each animal you see. Keep a tally on some paper. Each player also chooses themselves a bonus animal - a rare animal which will score them a bonus 10 points (e.g. a llama, a black pig, a white horse) If you pass a postbox on your side of the car you lose all your points.

TRY THIS!

Keep a travel journal and make entries each day. Stick in postcards, tickets and guides. Do little sketches of things that you see and do. Perhaps ask people you meet to write in your book.

20 Questions

Someone starts by thinking of a person, place or thing. Others ask questions that can be answered by 'yes' or 'no'. With strict rules, only 20 questions may be asked. If no-one guesses they get a point and try again. If you guess right it's your turn.

Never ending story

One person starts a story, takes the story to a cliffhanger and then passes over to the next. It's best played in three parts, with a different person in charge of beginning, middle and end. Make the stories as outrageous and silly as you can. Some starting suggestions could be: 'Mum turned into a flesh eating monster every night at 11...'; 'I first realised my pebble was magic when...'

Categories

One person thinks of a category, then take turns naming items that fit the category. If someone can't name something they are out. You mustn't repeat something another player has said. The game ends when one of the last two players can't continue. The other player gets a chance to name another thing. If they do they win. The harder the categories, the more fun. Tailor them to your children's interests, like 'horse breeds' or 'types of motorbikes'.

Alphabet Game

The classic alphabet game. Take it in turns to think of an animal starting with A, then B, and so on through the alphabet. For older children, try counties and states, countries, towns or cities, song titles and so on. Make the categories suit your children's interests. Or be about where you are travelling, like 'local towns and villages'.

TRY THIS!

One person hums the tune to a favourite TV show. The one who guesses right does the next song.

List game

Make a list before you leave on a long journey of things to spot along the way. You could style it like a bingo card. Use picture clues for younger children. Spot all of your list to win. Make different lists for different types of drive.

In the town:

- flashing light
- bus
- sign in a foreign language
- white dog
- video shop
- car advert
- policeman
- phone box
- person with a hat on
- pushchair

In the suburbs:

- school
- graveyard
- someone on a bike
- statue or clock
- church
- playground
- shopping trolley
- petrol station
- dog in a car
- GB sticker

TRY THIS!

Draw a list for toddlers

TODDLER 0–3 APPROVED

bike

bridge

green car

lorry

traffic lights

cow

postbox

hat

In the country:

- railway line
- post office
- cows
- pond or lake
- magpie
- tractor
- black and white dog
- horses
- windmill
- barn

Tin foil sculpture

Have a tube of foil in the car and give each child a large piece. See who can make the best sculpture. You can make bracelets, necklaces, animals, hats, wacky sunglasses, just about anything you can think of. The straight edges can be sharp, so warn them to take care, perhaps crumple it a bit before you give it to them.

Car Pool

Toss to see who's on yellow or red and who starts. If you spot a car in your colour it's a pot. Pot all seven balls in your colour, and then find a black car to win. But if the other player spots a white car, it's their turn to pot.

Hypochondria

This is an alphabet game, but you have to think of a disease or operation. Start with 'I went to hospital and had my Achilles tendon removed' then 'Brain scanned' and so on. At least X is an easy one in this game!

New I Spy

TODDLER 0-3 APPROVED

Everyone knows how to play I spy, but have you tried these variations? Try 'I spy something that rhymes with...' or if it's dark and you can't spy anything, try playing 'I'm thinking of...' instead.

TRY THIS!

Play guess the rhyme. One player thinks up a rhyming pair of words. Then that player gives a non-rhyming clue to the other players. For example big wig – large hairpiece.

Rock, paper, scissors

Put your hands behind your back and count 'One two, three', then bring out your hand in one of these three shapes. Scissors beats paper, rock beats scissors and paper beats rock.

Who's closest?

Who's closest? is a guessing game. One player thinks a random thought. The rest of the players then take turns trying to guess what they are thinking of. Once everyone has guessed the thinker reveals the actual thought and everyone takes it in turns to justify why they were closest. The thinker decides who was closest and that person becomes the next thinker. Unless a guess is really close, the decision is based mainly on how funny the justification is!

Map making

Make a map for your child to navigate home by. Walk with them but let them call the shots. Draw pictures and arrows if they are too young to read. Start off with a really simple one and then get more complicated.

Car cricket

Choose a batsman. They look out for pubs. They get a run (point) for each leg the pub's name has. For example, the 'Jolly Sailor' gets 2 points, the 'White Horse' gets 4. If a pub has no legs, the batsman is out and it is the next player's turn. You can adapt the rules, some players use the rule where any pub with the word 'arms' in the name scores 2 points. Alternatively, two players sitting on either side of the car play simultaneously scoring runs for the pubs passed on their side of the road.

The Queens Arms

TRY THIS!

To play this coin game, start with ten coins. The person who is 'it' hides several coins in their right hand and puts their hand in their lap. Everyone guesses how many coins there are. No one can guess the same number as someone else. The person who guesses correctly gets one point and becomes 'it'. The person with the most points after 15 minutes wins.

FizzBuzz

The aim of FizzBuzz is to count in turn. However, if any number is divisible by three it's replaced by the word Fizz, and if divisible by five, by the word Buzz. Numbers divisible by both become FizzBuzz. A player who hesitates or makes a mistake is out. Play continues until there is only one player left, the winner. For example 1, 2, Fizz, 4, Buzz, Fizz, 7, 8, Fizz, Buzz, 11, Fizz, 13, 14, FizzBuzz, and so on.

Songs to Sing

On Top of Spaghetti

On top of spaghetti
All covered with cheese,
I lost my poor meatball,
When somebody sneezed.

It rolled off the table
And onto the floor,
And then my poor meatball
Rolled out of the door.

It rolled in the garden
And under a bush,
And then my poor meatball
Was nothing but mush.
MUSH MUSH!

So if you eat spaghetti
All covered with cheese,
Hold onto your meatball
Lest somebody sneeze.

The wheels on the bus

The wheels on the bus go round and round
Round and round, round and round
The wheels on the bus go round and round
All day long.

TODDLER
0-3
APPROVED

The wipers on the bus go 'Swish, swish, swish'

The door on the bus goes open and shut

The horn on the bus goes 'Beep, beep, beep'

The baby on the bus says, 'Wah, wah, wah!'

The people on the bus say, 'Shh, shh, shh'.

On the Beach

Split into two teams. Each team has a cup and a bucket. Put both the buckets on the starting line. The first team member on each team rushes to the sea, fills their cups and races back to fill their buckets. Then the next members go in relay. The first full bucket wins.

Long John Silver's Treasure

Get an ice cream tub and fill it with 'treasure'; shells, copper coins, pretty pebbles, anything not living. One person buries the tub in the sand while the others aren't looking, (with a discreet marker stone or feather on top so you can find it again if the map fails!). Draw a map with a stick in the sand for the others use. See who can find Long John Silver's treasure first.

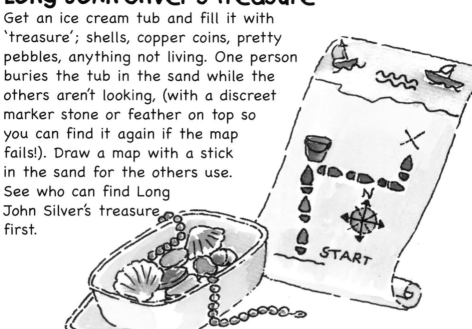

Coin on Coin

Get a bucket full of sea water. Drop a coin to the bottom, then drop a second coin and try and get the second to land on the first. Whoever covers the coin the best wins.

TRY THIS!

Collect beautiful stones and make a pebble picture on the sand. Take a photo of it to take home.

Always leave the pebbles on the beach.

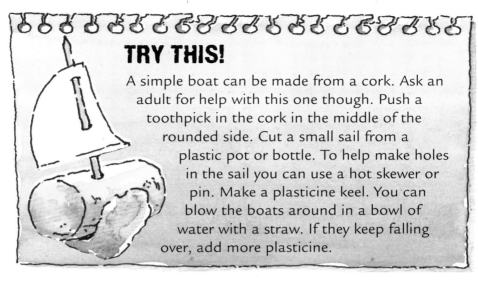

TRY THIS!

A simple boat can be made from a cork. Ask an adult for help with this one though. Push a toothpick in the cork in the middle of the rounded side. Cut a small sail from a plastic pot or bottle. To help make holes in the sail you can use a hot skewer or pin. Make a plasticine keel. You can blow the boats around in a bowl of water with a straw. If they keep falling over, add more plasticine.

Pebble tower

Collect pebbles and see who can build the tallest tower. Big, flat pebbles are best. If you build a really tall tower, take it down before you leave. It could hurt a little child if it fell.

Jumping race

Draw lines in the sand and see who can jump the furthest.

Limpet racing

Balance limpet shells upside down on your outstretched forefingers, or on your nose. Have races and see who can finish first without dropping their limpet. Make sure the route is clear of obstacles for the nose-balancing version. You can't look down!

Beach Scavenger Hunt

Each take a bucket and race to find a set list of objects. Perhaps a feather, the longest piece of sea weed, a stone with a stripe in it, a dogfish egg case, a mussel shell, a fossil, a piece of rope, a cuttle fish and some driftwood.

Throw it Backwards

Players line up side by side and one person moves out four feet in front. Keeping their back to all the other players they throw a ball backwards over their head. If the ball is caught, that person is the new thrower. If it's caught after a bounce, the catcher hides it behind their back. Everyone puts their hands behind their backs and asks the thrower to turn around and guess who has the ball. If correct, they get to throw again, but if the person with the ball isn't caught that player is the new thrower.

TRY THIS!

One person buries some numbered pieces of paper in a square marked out in the sand. The larger the number, the deeper you bury them in the sand. Then everyone races to dig them up again. The highest score wins. You could use shells instead, mussels could be 5 points and limpets, 10 points.

Beach combing crafts

Once you're back home, make these with your beach combing finds.

Driftwood sculpture

Some driftwood really looks like an animal or bird. You can make a sculpture by tying pieces together with rope, or use florists' oasis or playdough as a stand

Sand collage

Cut a sheet of dark paper to fit inside a box lid. Draw a picture with the tip of a glue bottle, then sprinkle on loose sand. Once the sand is dry, shake off the excess by gently tapping the side of the lid. Glue on shells or tiny pebbles to decorate.

TRY THIS!

Beach bingo is a fun game. Write a list of things to see, rather than collect, for example a man with hat, a black dog, a child with an ice-cream etc. The first one to tick off all the list wins. Draw pictures instead for the little ones who can't read very well.

Stone Skimming

Find a smooth, oval stone the size of the palm of your hand. It should be heavy enough not to get blown about, but light enough that you can throw it accurately. Calm water works best. Throw so the stone hits the water at the flattest possible angle, but ideally with the front side slightly higher than the rear. The best way is to throw the stone from a little above ankle height. Throw it fast with a good amount of spin. Get this with a flick of the wrist at the moment of release. Obviously don't throw near anyone in the water!

Keep the Box Full

You need a lot of tennis balls for this game, ideally two per player. Perhaps borrow some from neighbours on the beach? Get a box or bag and fill with the balls. One player takes it and has to roll the balls out one by one. The others have to chase after them and return them to the box. The idea is for the box never to empty.

If it does, the thrower scores one point and you change over.

TRY THIS!

Try making a small raft out of beach finds. Tie some driftwood together with seaweed or rope. Sail your raft in the shallows. Have races on the waves and see whose raft comes in the furthest up the beach.

Beach Bowling

All you need is a ball and a paper cup. Fill the cup with slightly damp sand and turn upside down to make the skittles. Make them in a triangle shape. Then bowl your ball at your handmade skittles. You could create two 'alleys' and race to see who can get them all down.

TRY THIS!

To play squirtball you need two beach balls and two water pistols or plastic water bottles with nozzle lids. Draw two goals in the sand. The players try to squirt the beach ball into the opposing player's goal, while guarding their own goal. The stronger the water jets, the better this game works. Enormous water guns work best if you have them. Don't squirt at people!

Sand Follow my Leader

Find an area of wet sand that holds footprints and other impressions well. While the other players close their eyes, one person creates a path of prints for the others to follow. Try walking backwards, doing a cartwheel, jumping. Take turns following the prints, fitting feet or hands as closely as possible into the impressions, and trying to work out how the path was made.

29

Rock Pooling

Exploring a rock pool is great fun. It is best to arrive just before low tide when the pools are clearly visible. Turn over rocks gently to reveal the life sheltering under it or actually living on the rock itself. Be careful and return the rock to exactly the same position and the same way up as you found it. If you place the rock back upside down, the attached life will die. You could find crabs, snails, prawns, starfish, sea anemones, barnacles, hermit crabs, seaweed, and fish. Some beaches will have information boards showing you the creatures you may find in the rock pools. Here are some to get you started.

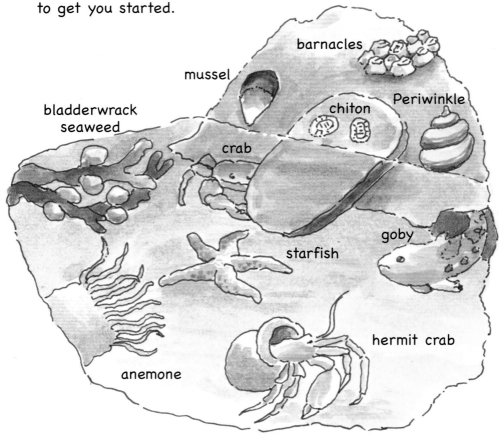

barnacles

mussel

chiton

Periwinkle

bladderwrack seaweed

crab

goby

starfish

hermit crab

anemone

Newspaper Boat

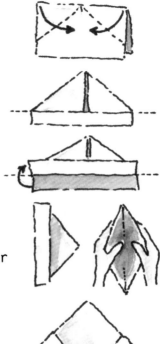

1. To make the boat, take a sheet of newspaper and fold a page in half, mark the middle and then fold down each side to make equal triangles.

2. Fold half the bottom strip upward on the dotted line.

3. Turn the paper over and fold the other lower strip upwards. You now have a paper hat.

4. Turn it and open it so you're looking inside the part you would wear on your head. The thumbs must be inside.

5. Lay the upper and the lower parts on each other so it looks like a diamond.

6. Fold the lower front triangle upwards along the dotted line. Turn the paper over and fold the other triangle up.

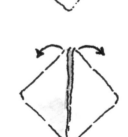

7. Open the hat again and flatten to make a diamond shape again. Pull the upper corners of the triangles in the direction of the arrows. Pull these corners and you'll see the boat forming before your eyes. Stretch the boat both to the right and left, and then separate it slightly from underneath so it can float.

Snail Croquet

Find a stick and a round pebble. Make a spiral in the sand with the stick.
Aim to hit the pebble from the opening to the centre without going over the line on to the other track. If the pebble goes over line, you have to start again.

Pebble Bowls

Collect two pebbles for each player. Make sure you can recognise yours. Get a smaller distinct pebble to act as the target. Toss the small pebble a good distance, then see who gets the closest with their pebbles. Don't throw near people!

Who Am I?

On a busy beach this is a fun game. Take it in turns to imitate someone. The others have to guess who you are mimicking. Chose someone who is moving, not sunbathing – or it may be hard for the others to guess! Make sure the person you are imitating can't see you though, or they may get annoyed!

Seaweed hairdressers

Collect a pile of seaweed. The cleanest will be closest to the sea as it will have been washed by the waves recently. Take it in turns to give each other elaborate hairstyles, plaits and all. Great fun particularly for balding dads. Wash your hands and head afterwards!

TODDLER
0-3
APPROVED

Sand Sculpture

It's easiest with really wet, compact sand. To sculpt, make a flat wet sand base, then build up a mound of compacted wet sand, built up out of piles of burger shaped 'sand patties' Then carve away to create your shape. Try making a giant's head in the sand, or a car. Beefburgers and hot dogs are quite easy, make the lettuce and meat from different colour seaweed.

Noughts and crosses toss

Draw a board in the sand and use stones or shells as the counters. The first player tosses a stone at the board. If it lands within a square, leave it on the board. If it is on the lines or off the board, take the stone away and the next players has a turn. Just like noughts and crosses, the object is to be the first one to finish a line of three pebbles.

TRY THIS!

Wrap a piece of newspaper into a cone and fill it with dry sand. Drip the sand through the hole to draw your picture. Or, fill a plastic cup with a 1cm hole in the bottom with sopping wet sand. You can make drawings, or dribble strange towers by dripping in the same place and gradually building it up.

Sand Mazes

Challenge each other with mazes drawn in the sand. Perhaps put a prize in the middle. If you scour a deep channel you will have a water maze for a while when the tide fills it.

Stuck in the Mud

One person is 'it'. Tagged people have to stand still with their legs apart. Others can release them by crawling through their legs. When all are 'stuck' someone else becomes it.

Against the tide

Split into teams and head down to the waters' edge with your buckets and spades. Each team needs to build a tall hard mound close to the incoming tide. Give yourselves ten minutes to build it. Then stand a team member on top of the mound, and see who can keep their balance the longest as the tide comes in. The last team with their mascot still standing on their team's 'castle', wins.

Bodyboarding

If there are breaking waves on the beach, bodyboarding is great fun. On many beaches you can hire or buy boards. Only bodyboard if you are a good swimmer, and if there are lifeguards present. Read the beach safety section on the inside front cover of this book first, and any safety information at the beach you are visiting. To catch a wave, lie on your board as the wave approaches and start paddling hard with your arms. The wave should catch you and push you along into the shore.

TEENAGER 10-15 APPROVED

In the Garden

On a fine night, try camping under the stars. You don't need a tent, a blanket over a washing line weighed down by a few stones will do. A disposable barbecue is fun to cook sausages and marshmallows on outside. Get an adult to help you cook. Perhaps sing campfire songs and tell spooky ghost stories.

Hot and Cold

Hide something in garden and get the others to try and find it. Say 'hot', 'warm', or 'cold' according to how close they are. 'Boiling hot' if they are standing right over it. See who finds it the quickest. You may want to whisper 'hot' or 'cold' in people's ears, otherwise if anyone hears a 'hot', they all rush over to the same place!

Nut Hunt

Hide a nut (or anything) in the garden and leave clues to find it. Create a trail of clues i.e. the first clue you hand to the child says 'go to tree', then have a note in tree saying 'go to patio'. For older children you could make the clues cryptic and harder to solve. Try mirror writing or codes.

TRY THIS!

Pavement art is fun. Do chalk drawings on the patio or driveway. The rain will wash them off. You can buy big pavement chalk, but normal chalk is fine. If you've got neither, you can just paint using a wet paintbrush. It'll dry away in the sunshine so there's no mess at all.

Bowling

Collect some empty plastic bottles, with lids. Half fill them with water or sand and arrange the bottles in a group. Perhaps upturn a table behind them to stop the ball rolling miles. Try and knock the bottles over with the ball.

Clock Golf

If you have a golf ball and putter around the house, this is a fun game for the family. Ask an adult to sink a tin can with a hole in the base in the ground, in the middle of the garden. Then put markers around the garden numbered one to twelve. Players start at one o'clock and try and putt the ball. Once you have potted it at one o'clock. move on to two o'clock and so on. The one with the least strokes is the winner.

Make your own golf putter

You can make a really simple golf club with two lengths of wood and two nails. You need a long piece of wood that is about as long as from your hips to the ground. Then you need a piece about 15cm long to be the blade. Get an adult to help you nail the two together.

TRY THIS!

Put a ball in a long sock or stocking. One person squats in the middle of a circle of players and swings the sock around. The circle have to jump over it. If anyone gets hit by the ball and sock, they are out and swap places with the person in the middle. You could use a skipping rope instead of the sock.

Dodge Ball

One or two players are the taggers. The taggers must hit the others on the legs with a ball. If someone is hit they sit down, but also join the taggers' team and are able to tag if they are thrown the ball. Once everyone's tagged, choose new taggers.

Limbless

Throw the ball round in a circle. If a player drops the ball they must get down on one knee; if they miss again they get down on two knees; then one arm goes behind their back, and finally, for a fourth miss, that person is out. If a successful catch is made, you go back up a stage.

Sevenses

Throw a ball against a wall seven times the first way, then six the next way and so on.

7 – Throw the ball against the wall and catch it with both hands.

6 – Throw the ball and catch with one hand only.

5 – Throw the ball and let it bounce once on the ground and catch it.

4 – Throw the ball under your leg against the wall and catch it.

3 – Throw the ball, clap your hands once, then catch.

2 – Throw the ball, turn around, let the ball bounce and catch.

1 – Throw the ball, let it bounce, bounce it again with the palm of your hand, scoop it up with the palm of your hand, then catch it.

Ball Games

TRY THIS!

Remember school sports day? Try staging a mini-olympics in the garden for fun. For the sack race use old pillow cases or a couple of strong big rubbish bags inside each other. Mark out a course and then try some of these other great events on this page too!

Egg and Spoon

Use potatoes or stones if you don't want to break your eggs. Balance them on a spoon and run.

Wheelbarrows

Pair up and one person is the barrow. The other holds the barrow's ankles and wheels them along. Race in pairs.

Fancy Dress Race

Split into two teams, and pile a hat, scarf, coat, wellies etc for each team a marked distance away. One player from each team must run to the end, put all the items on, and run back. They quickly undress, and dress the next team mate who runs to the marker and back. The first team back wins.

Limbo

Push two bean poles into the ground and tie a crossbar on with string. Slide the cross bar down a couple of centimetres once everyone has limboed at the first height. See who can get the lowest.

Welly Wanging

See who can throw a welly the furthest. Make sure you have a lot of space as this can be a dangerous one! For extra fun, fill the wellies with water.

Teddy's Picnic

Make little invitations and deliver them to all the teddies. Make party hats from newspaper (see p.31), Make tiny sandwiches: just use a sharp knife to cut a sandwich into little pieces. Iced gem biscuits make great cakes. Cut up tiny slices of carrot or cucumber. Lay the whole thing out on a picnic rug or tablecloth.

TODDLER 0-3 APPROVED

Knucklebones

Throw up a handful of small stones and see how many you can catch on the back of your hand.

Wall Game

Draw two parallel lines in the mud about a metre apart. This is the wall. One or two players stand between the lines. They are not allowed to go over these lines. The others have to run across the wall without being touched. If touched they must join the others on the wall. The last person caught is the next catcher on the wall.

Grass Whistle

Take a long, broad blade of grass and stretch it out between both thumbs pressed together side by side. Make sure it's held really taut. Blow hard through the gap and it should make a loud shriek.

TEENAGER 10-15 APPROVED

On a Rainy Day

*S*hipwreck is a fun game for a rainy day.
The floor is the shark-infested sea.
Scatter cushions on the floor and jump
around the room not touching the floor.
Gradually move all the islands further away
and see who touches the ground first.

Indoor Fort

Tables, duvets, tablecloths, chairs and cushions make a great fort. Make a pulley system with string and clothes pegs to send notes to each other. Tie a length of string from one bit of furniture to the other. Make sure it's OK with an adult first. Peg a note on to the string. Tie more string to the top of the peg, and have one end each. Pull the peg along the wire to get your mail, or anything else you can peg.

Charades

Write out on scraps of paper the titles of films, books and tv shows that your family know. Act out the titles, you mustn't speak. Either take it in turns, or whoever guesses right gets a turn.

TRY THIS!

TODDLER 0-3 APPROVED

No storybooks? No problem. Make up a story, and let the younger ones do the sound effects. Make sure your story includes lots of fun noises, like ice cream vans, piglets, mobile phones, windscreen wipers, lorries reversing, seagulls and so forth. Then swap over.

Ball Catchers

- 2 big plastic milk bottles or squash bottles
- Sharp scissors

Wash and dry the bottles well. Use the sharp scissors (grown ups only) to cut the bottle. First cut off the bottom, then cut a U shape under the handle. Make sure you don't cut into the handle. If you use them inside, use rolled up paper balls so you don't break anything.

Play Dough

It's really easy to make your
own play dough.

4 cups flour
1 cup salt
4 cups water
4 tablespoons oil
1/2 cup cream of tartar
Food colouring - perhaps
   make up a couple of
   different colours at a time in separate saucepans.
Vanilla essence - optional (improves the smell and texture)

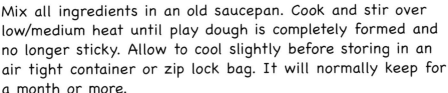

Mix all ingredients in an old saucepan. Cook and stir over
low/medium heat until play dough is completely formed and
no longer sticky. Allow to cool slightly before storing in an
air tight container or zip lock bag. It will normally keep for
a month or more.

Dough Game

A variation of the well known
drawing game - but instead of
using paper and pencil, play it
with play dough! Everyone
write down some things that
players have to model and put
them all in a hat to pull out.
Split into teams. One player
has to model the idea for
their team mates to guess.
Have some easy ones like
apple or pyramid, and some
hard ones like the Eiffel
tower.

TRY THIS!

Are you coordinated? Can
you pat your head and rub
your stomach at the same
time? Try writing the
number one in the air with
your right index finger and
write the number two in
the air with your left index
finger, then try doing that
at the same time, and
reverse the procedure. Try
going up to number ten.

Fortune Teller

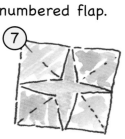

1. To make a square piece of paper, fold an A4 sheet like picture 1 and then cut off and discard the shaded area.

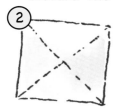

2. Fold in half diagonally twice and crease the paper so it looks like picture 2. Unfold so you are back to the square.

3. Next, fold each corner point into the centre. It should look like picture 3.

4. Next, flip it over and fold all four corners points into the centre again. It will look the same as 3 but smaller.

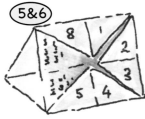

5. Write the numbers 1-8 on each of the triangles.

6. Lift up the flaps and write the fortunes under each numbered flap.

7. Flip it over and colour each flap.

8. Flip it back over and put your thumbs and forefingers into the four flap pockets. It should look like picture 8.

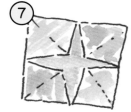

Ask a friend to choose a colour. Spell out the colour, and open and shut the fortune teller with each letter. Then ask for a number. Count out the number while opening and shutting again. The person picks a number one more time, and their fortune is under that flap.

School Steps

All you need are stairs and a coin or pebble. Decide who will be the teacher. The rest of the children sit on the first stair. The teacher puts their hands behind their back and puts the pebble in one hand. Go to the first child and have them guess which hand the pebble is in. If they guess correctly they go up a step. Teacher can switch the pebble for each player's turn if they choose. Whoever reaches the top stair first is the winner. The winner gets to be the teacher next game.

Air Ping Pong

TEENAGER 10-15 APPROVED

Spread the players around a table. With four players, assign each person one side of the table. Otherwise, decide what space around the table is each person's territory. Put a ping pong ball in the centre of the table. No one is allowed to touch the ball. They have to move it by blowing on it. A point is scored when the ball falls off the side of the table. The point goes to the person whose was guarding that territory. The winner is the person with the least number of points.

TRY THIS!

You need a large jar and a collection of clothes pegs. Put the jar on the floor and players in turn have to see how many pegs they can drop into the jar while they are standing over it. If it is too easy get them to stand on a chair. The person who gets the most pegs into the jar wins.

Animal Foldover

Each player has a strip of paper. Draw a head at the top and fold over so you can just see the neck. Pass the paper so the next person draws a body and so on. See what strange creatures you get.

TRY THIS!

Each person writes down a question beginning with 'why' (eg. 'Why is rain wet?'). Fold the top over to hide the question, and pass to the next person who, without looking at the question, writes an answer starting with 'because' (eg. 'Because pencils need sharpening'). Then read out all the questions and answers and see how silly they are.

Dice Code

Find two dice, pencils and paper. On your throw each player accumulates letters. Everyone is given a free letter B at the start.

1 = no letter   7 = D
2 = A   8 = H
3 = E   9 = N
4 = I   10 = S
5 = O   11 = T
6 = U   12 = Y

Keep throwing the dice until someone gets a five letter word.

Beetle

You need pencil and paper and a dice. The object is to complete your own beetle drawing. Whoever completes the beetle first wins. You need to throw a 1 to be able to start.

1 = draw the body
2 = draw the head
3 = draw the legs
4 = draw the eyes
5 = draw the feelers
6 = draw a tail

Battleships

Both players need two grids as shown. Write numbers across the top and letters down the side, so that the squares are easily identified as A7 or F5. One grid will be for plotting your own ships, the other for recording shots against your opponent's ships. Each player places 'ships' on his grid, of different sizes agreed by the players. One player will guess a square, their opponent will answer 'hit' or 'miss'. The first person to sink all the other person's ships wins.

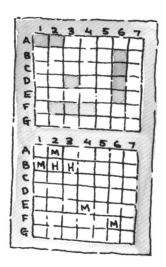

Word Puzzle

Each player makes their own 25 square grid. Take it in turns to shout out a letter. You can put it anywhere on the grid. The object is to make as many 3 letter or more words as possible.

Scribbles

Draw a continuous line scribble, then colour in the shapes, or try to make pictures from the shapes.

Chocolate Game

You need a dice, a hat, thick gloves or oven gloves, scarf, a bar of chocolate in its wrapper, a plate, a knife and fork. Players take turns to throw the dice. On throwing a six, put on the clothes and gloves before picking up the knife and fork. Attempt to get into the chocolate bar and eat it using the knife and fork only. Meanwhile the others keep throwing the dice. The next player who throws a 6 pulls off the hat and gloves and it's their turn.

ON A RAINY DAY

First Lines

Pick a book at random. Read out the title and a brief summary of it from the flyleaf. Then write down the real first line, and all the other players write down a made up first line. Collect the papers and read them out. Read them again, this time allowing votes to be cast for the most convincing. The most voted-for line author gets two points, anybody guessing the real first line gets one point.

Boxes

Draw a grid of dots on some paper. Draw a line connecting two adjacent dots. The second player then draws another line to connect another two dots. The goal is to be the person who draws the last side of a square. Put your initials inside the square and keep the turn until you can't complete any more boxes. The player with the most squares at the end is the winner.

Flour Game

Things do get messy with this game so be warned! On a large plate, make a mound of flour. Give it a flat top and lay a sweet on top of this. Using a blunt knife, take it in turns to remove sections of flour. If a person causes the sweet to fall into the flour they have to pick it out using their mouth only! Make sure they don't breathe in the flour or choke on the sweet though. Not suitable for tots.

TRY THIS!

You need some peas, a plate and cup and a straw. Time each player trying to move as many peas as possible from the plate into a cup by sucking through the straw. The player moving the most peas by the end of the game wins. You could try races if you get a straw and cup each.